LIFE

KATHARINE HEPBURN

1907 — 2003

Published by

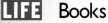
LIFE Books

Time Inc.
1271 Avenue of the Americas,
New York, NY 10020

ISBN: 1-932273-15-8

"LIFE" is a trademark of Time Inc.

We welcome your comments and
suggestions about LIFE Books.
Please write to us at:
LIFE Books, Attention:
Book Editors, PO Box 11016,
Des Moines, IA 50336-1016

If you would like to order any of
our hardcover Collector's Edition
books, please call us at
1-800-327-6388 (Monday through
Friday, 7:00 a.m.– 8:00 p.m. or
Saturday, 7:00 a.m.–6:00 p.m.
Central Time).

Please visit us, and sample past
editions of LIFE, at www.LIFE.com.

Iconic images from the LIFE Picture Collection are now available as
fine art prints and posters. The prints are reproductions on archival,
resin-coated photographic paper, framed in black wood, with an
acid-free mat. Works by the famous LIFE photographers—
Eisenstaedt, Parks, Bourke-White, Burrows, among many others—
are available. The LIFE poster collection presents large-format,
affordable, suitable-for-framing images. For more information on the
prints, priced at $99 each, call 888-933-8873 or go to
www.purchaseprints.com.
The posters may be viewed and ordered at www.LIFEposters.com.

This book, *Katharine Hepburn: 1907–2003,* was produced by the
LIFE editorial and publishing staff, and is published by LIFE Books
and Time Inc. Home Entertainment.

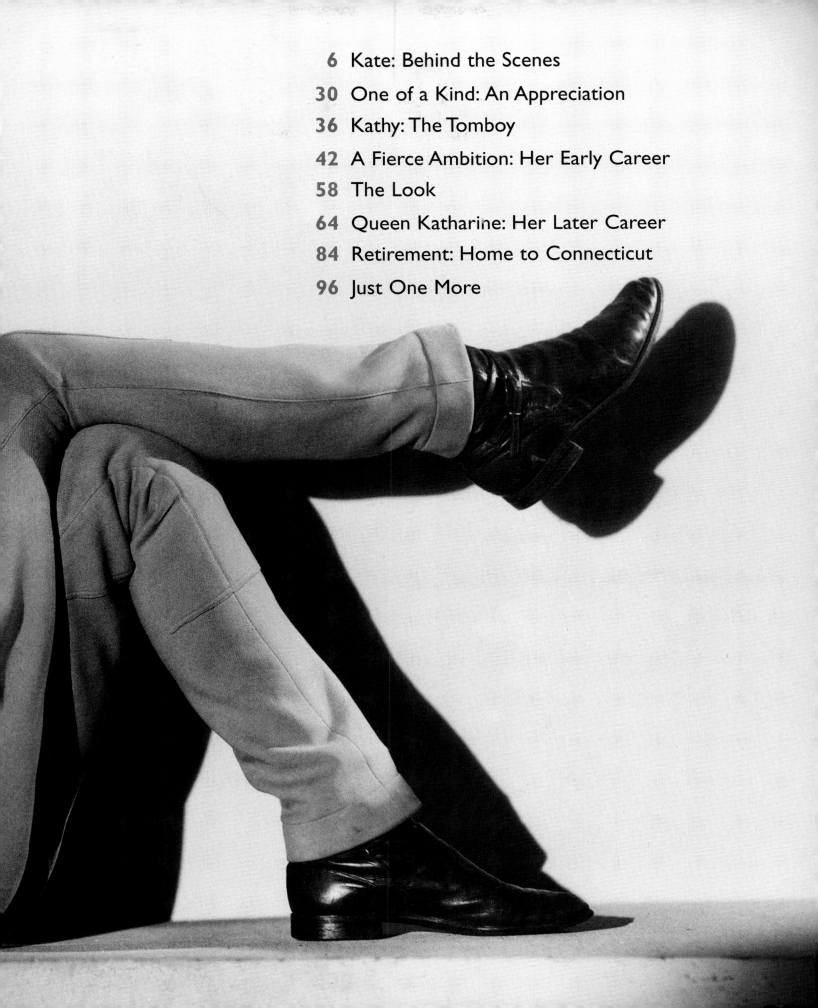

HEPBURN AT 27, IN 1934. "THE CURIOUS THING IS, WHEN I STARTED OUT, I DIDN'T HAVE ANY GREAT DESIRE TO BE AN ACTRESS OR TO LEARN HOW TO ACT," SHE SAID. "I JUST WANTED TO BE FAMOUS."

KATE

On THE SET OF *ALICE ADAMS*, 1935, WITH COSTAR FRED MACMURRAY. HER PERFORMANCE AS A SMALL-TOWN GIRL DESPERATELY TRYING TO BE CLASSY WON HER AN ACADEMY AWARD NOMINATION.

W ITH HOWARD HUGHES, IN 1935. AS ENERGETIC AS THE MOVIE STAR, HUGHES WOULD BREAK A WORLD SPEED RECORD PILOTING HIS PLANE. THE COUPLE TRIED TO HIDE THEIR RELATION-SHIP FROM THE WORLD, AND HEPBURN LATER WROTE: "I WAS HAPPY WITH HIM BECAUSE, LIKE ME, HE WAS A 'STAY-AT-HOME.'"

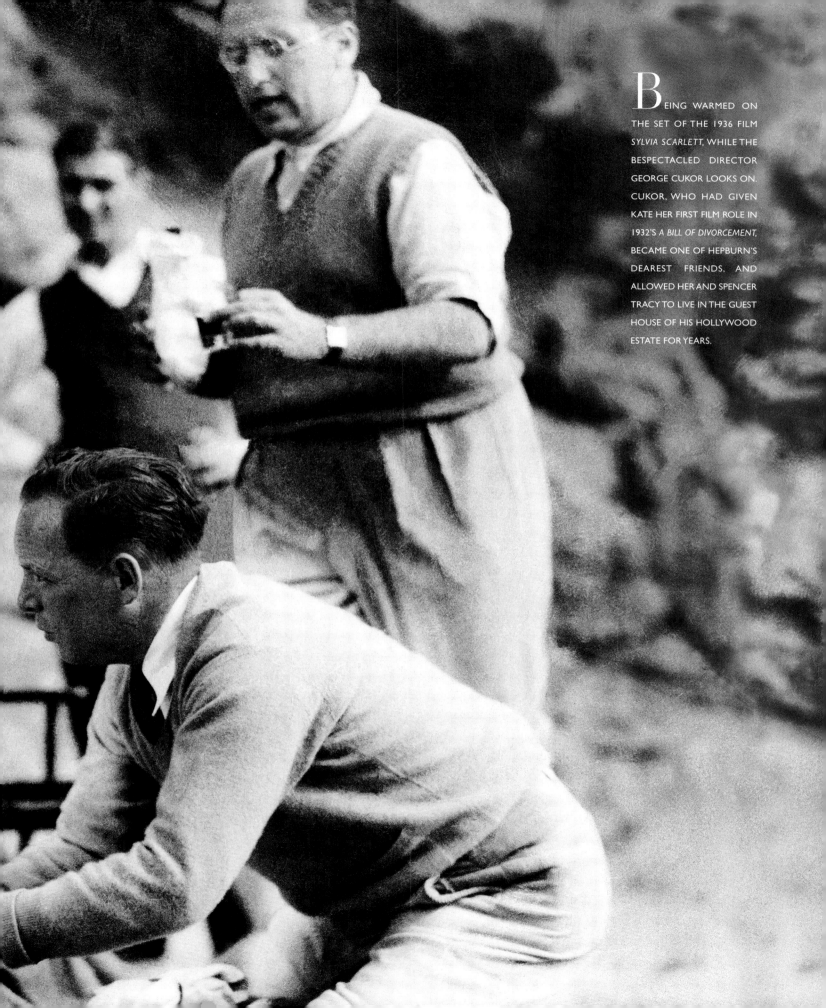

BEING WARMED ON THE SET OF THE 1936 FILM *SYLVIA SCARLETT*, WHILE THE BESPECTACLED DIRECTOR GEORGE CUKOR LOOKS ON. CUKOR, WHO HAD GIVEN KATE HER FIRST FILM ROLE IN 1932'S *A BILL OF DIVORCEMENT*, BECAME ONE OF HEPBURN'S DEAREST FRIENDS, AND ALLOWED HER AND SPENCER TRACY TO LIVE IN THE GUEST HOUSE OF HIS HOLLYWOOD ESTATE FOR YEARS.

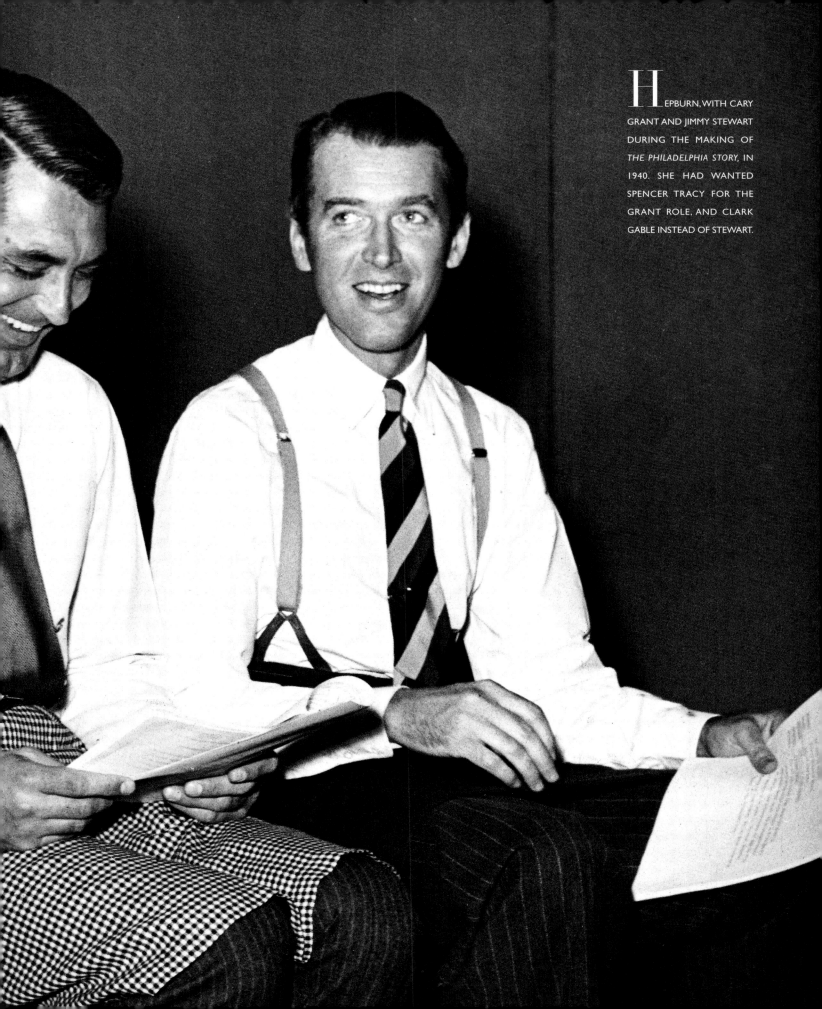

O N THE SET OF *THE IRON PETTICOAT*, IN 1956. HEPBURN SPARRED WITH HER COSTAR, BOB HOPE, AND LATER SAID SHE REGRETTED HAVING MADE THE MOVIE.

DISTINCTLY OUT OF CHARACTER, HEPBURN DURING A BREAK FROM THE DEMANDING ROLE OF DRUG-ADDICTED MARY TYRONE IN 1962'S *LONG DAY'S JOURNEY INTO NIGHT*. ONLY SHORTLY BEFORE FILMING THE EUGENE O'NEILL DRAMA, SHE HAD RECONNECTED WITH THE THEATER, APPEARING ON THE BOARDS IN SEVERAL OF SHAKESPEARE'S PLAYS.

PETER O'TOOLE AND
HEPBURN, ON THE SET OF
THE LION IN WINTER, 1968.
ONLY MONTHS AFTER TRACY
HAD DIED, HEPBURN MOVED
ON WITH LIFE. PLAYING
A GLEEFUL ELEANOR OF
AQUITAINE, SHE HAD GREAT
FUN NEEDLING O'TOOLE.

HEPBURN AND JOHN WAYNE, FILMING *ROOSTER COGBURN*, 1975. THE DUKE'S ASSESSMENT OF HIS COSTAR: "DAMN! THERE'S A WOMAN."

Gertrude

RELAXING WITH HER DEAR FRIEND HENRY FONDA DURING THE FILMING OF 1981'S *ON GOLDEN POND*. AS ETHEL THAYER, A SPIRITED WOMAN SEIZING EACH AND EVERY DAY FOR HER AND HER FRAIL HUSBAND, HEPBURN ALLOWED HER OFFSCREEN PERSONA AND EMOTIONS TO IMBUE HER NUANCED, MOVING PERFORMANCE.

SECRETARY PHYLLIS
WILBOURN AND HEPBURN,
IN THE KITCHEN, DURING
THE TWILIGHT YEARS. SAID
EMPLOYER OF EMPLOYEE:
"SHE IS A TOTALLY SELFLESS
PERSON WORKING FOR A
TOTALLY SELFISH PERSON."

HEPBURN AT HER FAMILY HOME AFTER A PLUNGE IN THE OCEAN ON A 5° DAY. SHE ONCE SAID, "NOT EVERYONE IS LUCKY ENOUGH TO UNDERSTAND HOW DELICIOUS IT IS TO

One
of a
Kind

BY **MARILYN JOHNSON**

"I COULD ONLY IMAGINE MYSELF IN ALL THE LEADING PARTS. . . .I FELT THEY W

K

atharine Hepburn is coming out of the icy surf of Long Island Sound on a bitterly cold day in February, running toward Fenwick, her beloved family home. This picture may be the most revealing one ever taken of her. All we see is her back, but we can tell she's fit and hardy, this octogenarian, fresh from her daily swim and waving her towel like a flag. She couldn't have been more passionate or arrogant. As John Wayne said of her, "Yes, sir, she's tough. Christ! She wants to do everything!"

She lived at full throttle for most of a century; she was nearly as old as the movies. She cut a swath through 60 years of motion picture history, and her 47 films left incandescent proof of her life force. She was the fast-talking independent woman who spun circles around Cary Grant and Spencer Tracy and Jimmy Stewart; the aging missionary with the bold heart who fell in love with Humphrey Bogart's drunk riverboat captain in *The African Queen;* the morphine-addicted mother who whipsawed between sweetness and rage in *Long Day's Journey Into Night;* the banished old queen plotting against her young husband in *The Lion in Winter.* These were her great parts, but she also played ingenues, boys, a Chinese girl, spinsters—and she had an ambitious stage career that included a triumphant turn as Coco Chanel. She never played a whore, never got to play her dream role, Scarlett O'Hara. Although Tennessee Williams wrote *The Night of the Iguana* for her, she turned it down. In real life she appeared as the eccentric actress Katharine Hepburn, wearing old pants and a torn shirt, her hair flying, smoking a cigarette—a blunt Yankee aristocrat who

1933

1933

Y TO HAVE ME. THE FACT THAT I'D DONE PRACTICALLY NOTHING NEVER OCCURRED TO ME. 99

encompassed parts of all these characters. In many ways, being herself was her greatest role.

In her early years she looked as ravishing as Garbo, all cheekbones and lithe movement. An athlete, she was still in peak form at the age of 45, when she golfed, biked, swam and even boxed her way through *Pat and Mike*. As she aged and weathered, as her hands and head began to shake with palsy, she would bring these elements to her roles. After she jumped into a Venice canal for a stunt in *Summertime* and contracted incurable conjunctivitis, she used her perpetually watering eyes to sentimental advantage in *Guess Who's Coming to Dinner?* and *On Golden Pond*. Within a year of getting a hip replaced, she made a movie on horseback with John Wayne, who had just lost a lung. They were both 68, both wounded, yet each still tried to upstage the other. Hepburn was fighting for the role of preeminent actress of the century—as if there was any question.

1934

1934

1935

She was a red-haired, densely freckled wild girl. Maybe a wild boy, too. She called herself Jimmy and just for a thrill used to break into houses with a pal from her Hartford neighborhood. She was untamed, at home in the tops of trees.

She had only a few friends when she was growing up and, in all the world, was closest to her older brother, Tom. They lived in a tumultuous house with four younger siblings, a mother who was a prominent feminist—she helped found the organizations that became Planned Parenthood and the League of Women Voters—and a dominating father who was a surgical pioneer in urology and used to stroll around the house naked. Everyone was always yelling and arguing politics. The Hepburn parents battled social problems that most people in the early part of this century didn't even talk about, and the Hepburn children discussed venereal disease and prostitution and birth control at the kitchen table. The family was all but shunned in Hartford. Their people, their friends, were some of the great social reformers of that time: Emma Goldman, Charlotte Perkins Gilman, Emmeline Pankhurst, Sinclair Lewis, Margaret Sanger. But for all their liberal ways, the Hepburn parents believed in physical discipline. "Were we spanked?" Hepburn once said with pride. *"Beaten."*

When she was 13, she found Tom's body hanging from the rafters in his godmother's house in New York City, where the children had been spending a vacation. It was a tragedy that changed her life completely. "It was as if, when Tom died, I sort of became two people instead of one—a boy and a girl." The wild girl turned moody and withdrawn, dropped out of school and was tutored at home, her parents almost her only companions until she left for Bryn Mawr at 17, in 1924.

The first time she walked into the college cafeteria, an older girl pointed her out as a "self-conscious beauty." Mortified, Hepburn ate in her room after that, and for the rest of her life avoided eating in public. (She always had a healthy appetite. "That girl can eat," Garson Kanin once said.) A strange young woman in wrinkled clothes—but flamboyant, in spite of her shyness (she once swam nude in the school fountain)—Hepburn floundered until she discovered acting. She won the lead in a school production. Cast as a boy, she pulled on a pair of pants and a tie and began to live

❝IF YOU DON'T DREAM UP YOUR PARENTS, YOUR BROTHERS AND SISTERS, YOUR FRIENDS, AND THE PER

Her early career was rocky. When she did land parts in plays, she got overexcited and raced through her lines. She was fired frequently. In New York City she understudied a boyish actress of the late '20s named Hope Williams in the play *Holiday*. But she was not destined to be an understudy, and in 1928, for the first but not the last time, Katharine Hepburn turned her back on acting. Her break lasted the length of her honeymoon with a Main Line heir, Ogden Ludlow, who dropped his last name, Smith, at Hepburn's request. (The marriage quickly collapsed, but Ludlow remained Hepburn's friend all his life.) By 1932, working steadily again, she won the role of an Amazon in *The Warrior's Husband* on Broadway. She created a sensation when she strode onstage with a stag draped over her shoulders, eclipsing Hope Williams in boyishness and, soon, fame. "I incorporated a lot of Hope into my so-called personality," she said. "It was in the air, that boy-woman."

She went to Hollywood and performed her screen test for RKO with her back to the camera—a bold gambit that worked. She later said that all the other actresses had to read the same boring scene, and she had stood out merely because she was different. Director George Cukor disagreed: "The camera focused on her back. There was an enormous feeling, a *weight*," particularly when she picked up a glass of champagne and turned at last to the camera.

She became a star with her first picture, *A Bill of Divorcement,* and won the 1933 Best Actress Oscar with her third, *Morning Glory*. But during the next few years, her movies were not well received, even though they included such classics as *Holiday* (in Hope Williams's role, which Hepburn had coveted) and the hilariously suggestive *Bringing Up Baby,* both with Cary Grant. The 1936 *Sylvia Scarlett,* another film with Grant, was a financial disaster. After she was labeled "box office poison" by theater owners, she quit Hollywood and went home. In 1940 she battled back with *The Philadelphia Story,* a script written for her, to which she owned the film rights, compliments of her close friend Howard Hughes. *The Philadelphia Story,* a smash, changed everything.

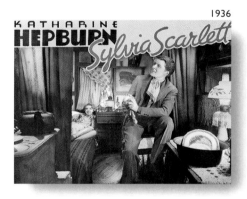

She created in films and theater a fresh new image for women—outspoken, ambitious, smart and equal, or nearly equal, to men. Though her movies with Spencer Tracy seem dated now, their battles of wit still spark. Even a confection like *Desk Set* can be seen as revolutionary: She makes a middle-aged, single, superintelligent research librarian into a funny, sexy leader. And yet her mother, the feminist, didn't see her as a feminist at all; her mother thought films were "silly" and showed little interest in Katharine's work until she did Shakespeare and Shaw onstage.

Hepburn was nominated for 12 Best Actress Oscars and won four, but she never attended the Academy Awards as a nominee. In fact, she was indifferent to most of the rewards of celebrity, hated to walk down the street, refused to give autographs and once, in a car surrounded by fans, commanded the chauffeur: "Drive on. We'll sweep up the blood later!"

She was much like Howard Hughes, one of her numerous conquests. They dated for three years and lived together in 1937 in his house next to the Wilshire Country Club in Los Angeles, where they could jump the fence to play golf. They adored the game. Each was ambitious, private,

T YOU LOVE—IF YOU JUST SEE THEM IN TOTAL FOUR-LETTER-WORD REALITY, THEN GOD HELP YOU. "

eccentric and obsessed with cleanliness. (Hepburn bathed as many as eight times a day, in cold water; Hughes's fear of germs eventually turned him into a recluse.) Both were daredevils, and he taught her how to fly. "It seems to me now that we were too similar," Hepburn reflected later. "We'd been brought up in ease. We each had a wild desire to be famous."

Many of the people Hepburn was close to had a hand in her career. Hughes bankrolled crucial films. The agent Leland Hayward, with whom she had an affair, helped her get money and clout at a time when actors, as studio property, could not demand much of either. Laura Harding, the American Express heiress who abandoned her acting career to accompany Hepburn to Hollywood and who lived with her for years, taught Hepburn how to play dashing heiresses. Spencer Tracy taught her how to simplify.

Hepburn avoided the Hollywood social scene, except on her own peculiar terms. She and Harding once snuck into a dinner party dressed as maids. She and producer Irene Selznick used to swim across town, hopping backyard to backyard, helping themselves to other people's pools. Her constant companion of 40 years was not some fellow actor but her secretary, Phyllis Wilbourn.

On sets, Hepburn preferred the company of the crew and her producers and directors to that of other actors. She said, "My father always advised an impersonal relationship with fellow workers"—a rule of thumb adopted by this dutiful daughter from a faraway time. According to John Barrymore, Hepburn spurned a pass from him on the set of her first movie by saying, "No! No! Please! My father doesn't want me to have any babies." Barrymore subsequently described her as "a creature most strange. A nut." The feeling was mutual: "What an odd man," she said of him. She found Henry Fonda, too, "an oddie. I never felt that I knew him at all." She admired Humphrey Bogart but thought he was another "odd fellow." Bogart called her "either a twenty-four-carat nut, or a great actress working mighty hard at being one." "She is terrifying," said Peter O'Toole. "It is sheer masochism working with her. She has been sent by some dark fate to nag and torment me." Of course, O'Toole had his own reputation for wreaking havoc on sets, and his kind of fun wouldn't have been Hepburn's. She would go to bed early to avoid parties like those described in her book *The Making of the African Queen: or How I Went to Africa with Bogart, Bacall and Huston and Almost Lost My Mind,* in which everyone sat around drinking and howling over a monkey who "leaped about and bit people and drank their drinks . . . it just seemed to me entirely stupid." As it was, no doubt.

And yet she was drawn to drinkers. She loved the director John Ford, who could not bring himself to leave his wife for her and who used to hole up in a room for days at a time, drinking. She loved the actor Spencer Tracy, who would not divorce his wife for her and who used to lock himself in a room for days at a time, drinking—while she kept vigil on the floor outside his door. She preferred to sit at Tracy's feet; she adored his talent, his humor and his domineering, even cruel style. She loved sparring with him. "A reasonable facsimile of Dad," one of her brothers observed.

661 I CAN ONLY SAY I THINK THAT IF [TRACY] HADN'T LIKED ME, HE WOULDN'T HAVE HUNG AROUND

She tailored her movie schedule, her ambitions, her personality and her clothes to suit Tracy. It was after she met him that she began wearing elegant pantsuits, for instance, instead of torn khakis. In 1962, after she filmed *Long Day's Journey Into Night*, she dropped out of the business for five years to devote herself to nursing him; the two of them disappeared, though they could be spotted from time to time flying kites in the canyons of Los Angeles. She talked him into one last movie, *Guess Who's Coming to Dinner?* and played many of her scenes to an empty wall so he could rest. For the length of their 27-year relationship, Tracy lived alone, with neither his wife nor his mistress. But at the end of Tracy's life, when he was clearly dying, Hepburn slept in the maid's room.

While Tracy was alive, Hepburn rarely talked to the press, but after his death she opened up a bit. She let the photographer John Bryson record her life at home; she hosted a television tribute to Tracy; she published an autobiography, *Me*, in which she confessed, "I have no idea how Spence felt about me." The man she said "I would have done anything for" was ultimately a mystery to her. "Who was he? I never really knew. And he is the only one who ever knew me."

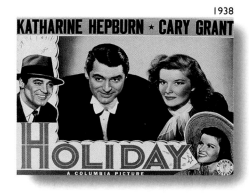

1938
KATHARINE HEPBURN ★ CARY GRANT
HOLIDAY
A COLUMBIA PICTURE

The only other people she adored unquestioningly were her parents, and she stayed her parents' child her whole life. After she became a star, she sent all her money home to be invested by her father, who sent her back an allowance. She never bought a house in California, though she lived most of her life there, renting. When she was on the East Coast, she went to her family's home every weekend, and when she was on location, she propped pictures of her mother and father by her bedside. She never had children of her own. "I would have made a terrible parent," she said once. "The first time my child didn't do what I wanted, I'd kill him."

The Hepburns had always refused to talk about their son Tom after his death. In a house in which anything else could be discussed, the family suicides—and there were others, including those of Hepburn's grandfather and three uncles—were taboo. But Katharine forgave her parents their silence. "They moved on into life," she explained. "They simply did not believe in moaning about anything." As for herself, she only wondered: Had Tom told her, the evening before, that she was his favorite girl, or had she fantasized it?

1940
CARY GRANT · KATHARINE HEPBURN · James STEWART
The Philadelphia Story
RUTH HUSSEY   JOHN HOWARD / ROLAND YOUNG / JOHN HALLIDAY / MARY NASH / VIRGINIA WEIDLER   BROADWAY'S HOWLING YEAR-RUN COMEDY HIT OF THE SNOOTY SOCIETY BEAUTY WHO SLIPPED AND FELL... IN LOVE!

The one thing Katharine Hepburn ever did against her parents' wishes was become an actress. Her mother was indifferent, her father "disgusted and heartsick" at her decision, Hepburn remembered—"thought it a silly profession closely allied to streetwalking." And perhaps this is why she so outdid herself: coming earlier and staying later than anyone else on the set, the fiercest competitor, the consummate professional who knew everybody's jobs better than they, who could step into roles with a weekend's notice, who performed on film, stage and television, in comedies, tragedies and musicals, winning more awards than anyone, outlasting generations of actors—an original, with the heart and soul of a reckless and boyish girl, always poised to stride off into the sunset, trousers flapping, showing us her beautiful and eloquent back.

1942
SPENCER TRACY · KATHARINE HEPBURN   THE PICTURE OF THE YEAR!
Woman of the Year
A GEORGE STEVENS Production
FAY BAINTER · REGINALD OWEN

Katharine Houghton Hepburn: She was named for her mother, a woman who taught her to speak her own mind, hold her ground and, paradoxically, how to submit to a domineering man. From her father she inherited red hair and an urge to compete physically, even recklessly.

Her mother had come from money but had been orphaned at 16. She'd had to fight for her inheritance, and thereby the right to determine her own future. Thomas Hepburn's bloodlines could be traced to the Scottish Earl of Bothwell, but he was the son of an American preacher who earned barely a pittance. Hard lives, a shared sense of entitlement and a powerful physical attraction cemented the union of Katharine and Thomas, who wed in 1904. Together, they fought to promote discussion of such stigmatized subjects as venereal disease and birth control. Yet they refused to acknowledge the suicidal depressions that had already claimed members in each of their families and that would eventually claim their oldest son, Tom.

Kathy, their second-oldest child, was born in 1907. A rough-and-tumble girl, she cut off her hair and called herself Jimmy. She used to tie her sled to the bumper of her father's car and fly through the streets. She was so wild she stood out even at radical gatherings. "I want her to express her true self, fully!" her mother said as the eight-year-old rampaged through the room, grabbing food from people's plates. "We never suppress her."

Kathy was only 13 when she found her older brother's body hanging in the attic, his neck broken by a noose made of sheets. Afterward, she hid from the world; the old Kathy disappeared. Kate emerged years later on the Bryn Mawr stage, a meld of Kathy and Tom, a strange, fierce girl who would live more than one person's life at a time.

THE STOWE-DAY FOUNDATION

"I'M LIKE THE GIRL WHO NEVER GREW UP, YOU SEE. I JUST NEVER LEFT HOME. I'VE ALWAYS COME BACK."

HEPBURN'S CHILDHOOD WAS SPENT IN THE FAMILY'S WELL-APPOINTED HOMES IN HARTFORD. "NEIGHBORS WOULD CALL UP AND SAY, 'KATHY'S SITTING IN THE TOP OF A TREE,'" REMEMBERED HEPBURN. "AND MOTHER WOULD SAY, 'WELL FOR HEAVEN'S SAKE DON'T FRIGHTEN HER.'"

"I loved Dad and Mother. They always had the last word with me. If they wanted it—I did it. And happily . . . they loved me—and I felt this and it made me very happy. They brought us up with a feeling of freedom. There were NO RULES. There were simply certain things which we did—and certain things which we didn't."

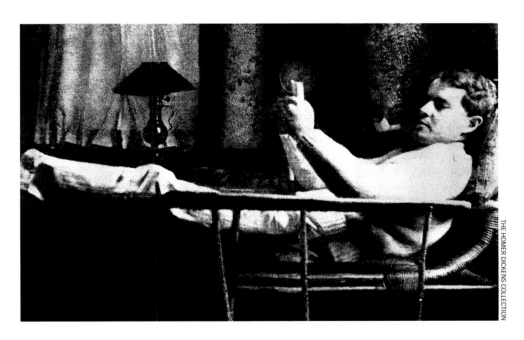

KATHY, HER MOTHER AND HER SIB-LINGS POSED (OPPOSITE) IN 1921—KATHY HOLDING SISTER MARI-ON, MOTHER HOLDING PEG. THE BOYS ARE (FROM LEFT) BOB, TOM AND DICK; TOM KILLED HIMSELF SOON AFTER THIS PHOTOGRAPH WAS TAKEN. ABOVE: DR. TOM HEPBURN IN 1913. STINGY WITH COMPLIMENTS, HE ASSUMED HIS CHIL-DREN WOULD EXCEL AT EVERYTHING.

PHOTOFEST

" I tried school but it was—well, I should say I was—I felt isolated. I knew something that the girls did not know: tragedy. **"**

Hepburn gained confidence as a collegian, class of '28. As a freshman she was "just painfully self-conscious," but "my last three years at Bryn Mawr were nowhere near as traumatic." In 1939, one year after *Holiday* and *Bringing Up Baby*—now classics—had flopped, actress Kate posed with lookalike sisters Marion (opposite, top left) and Peg (top right). ☐

"I know of no one who has ever remained indifferent to Katharine Hepburn.'
—GARSON KANIN

True enough. From Tallulah Bankhead, who knelt weeping at Hepburn's feet after having seen *Little Women,* to Dorothy Parker, who said about her performance in *The Lake,* "She ran the gamut of emotions from A to B." . . . From an audience electrified by a wordless scene she played in *A Bill of Divorcement,* to a stampede for the exits when, dressed as a boy in *Sylvia Scarlett,* she kissed a girl. . . . From John Barrymore, who tried to romance her and remembered every hour filming her first movie, to Adolphe Menjou, who volunteered to the House Un-American Activities Committee, "Scratch a do-gooder, like Hepburn, and they'll yell 'Pravda!'" . . . From Broadway to Hollywood and back again, Katharine Hepburn had the power to stir people.

"She was this slip of a woman—skinny, and I never liked skinny women," Cary Grant recalled. "But she had this thing, this air, you might call it, the most totally magnetic woman I'd ever seen and probably have ever seen since. You had to look at her, you had to listen to her, there was no escaping her."

On the set of *Stage Door,* her costar Lucille Ball griped: "Have you ever noticed something? How every time she gets into a new scene, no matter where, or on what stage, and she's wearing a new outfit, every son-of-a-bitch on this lot , from every department, finds his way over there—or her way—to stand around and gawk? Why is that? I notice they don't do it for any of the rest of us. Only for her."

SPRINGER/CORBIS-BETTMANN

" GET ME A BOWL OF WATER, WILL YOU! I'M IN A TERRIFIC SWEAT! " —KH AS ANTIOPE

IN 1927 AT BRYN MAWR (ABOVE, SECOND FROM RIGHT) HEPBURN APPEARED IN *THE TRUTH ABOUT BLAYDS,* A PLAY BY A.A. MILNE. FIVE YEARS LATER SHE CREATED A SENSATION ON BROADWAY IN *THE WARRIOR'S HUSBAND* (OPPOSITE).

" I WANT TO BE AN ACTRESS. I WANT TO LEARN EVERYTHING. "

HEPBURN ARRIVED IN PASADENA BY TRAIN IN 1932 (ABOVE) AND REPORTED TO THE RKO LOT TO BEGIN FILMING *A BILL OF DIVORCEMENT* WITH JOHN BARRYMORE (RIGHT). DAVID O. SELZNICK, WHO HAD SIGNED HER, RECALLED THAT "WHEN THE FIRST RUSHES WERE SHOWN, THE GLOOM AROUND THE STUDIO WAS SO HEAVY YOU COULD CUT IT WITH A KNIFE. 'YE GODS, THAT HORSE FACE!' "

"To win her, to beat down that proud, impervious hauteur, is a challenge only the most virile and dominant male could afford to take up. That's the sort of man who should play opposite her. And if he were strong enough to make her melt—oh, that would be worth filming.**"**

—Director Gregory La Cava

HEPBURN PLAYED AN AVIATRIX IN HER SECOND FILM, 1933'S *CHRISTOPHER STRONG* (OPPOSITE). SHE WON AN ACADEMY AWARD THAT YEAR FOR PLAYING A HUNGRY ACTRESS IN *MORNING GLORY* (TOP); HER COSTAR WAS ADOLPHE MENJOU, WHOM SHE DETESTED. *SPITFIRE* (CENTER) WAS ABOUT AN OZARK MOUNTAIN GIRL WHO BECOMES AN OUTCAST. *THE LITTLE MINISTER* (BOTTOM), IN WHICH SHE PLAYED A FREE-SPIRITED GYPSY, APPEARED IN 1934.

"LITTLE WOMEN. A BRILLIANT SCRIPT, SIMPLE AND TRUE AND NAIVE BUT REALLY BELIEVABLE. . . . THE SETS WERE LOVELY, COPIES OF THE ORIGINAL IN MASSACHUSETTS. THIS PICTURE WAS HEAVEN TO DO. IT WAS TO ME MY YOUTH!"

HEPBURN POSES ON THE SET OF *LITTLE WOMEN* IN 1933 ALONGSIDE DOUGLASS MONTGOMERY. THE FILM WAS A CRITICAL SUCCESS AND A HIT AT THE BOX OFFICE; THE ROLE, SAID HEPBURN, WAS THE MOST AUTOBIOGRAPHI-CAL OF HER CHARACTERS.

"PEOPLE WHO WANT TO BE FAMOUS ARE REALLY LONERS. OR THEY SHOULD BE."

WHEN HEPBURN WENT TO PARIS WITH A FEMALE AC-QUAINTANCE IN 1933, SHE HID IN HER STATEROOM WHILE REPORTERS POUNDED ON THE DOOR. SHE WAS MORE COOPERATIVE A SHORT TIME LATER WHEN SHE RETURNED ALONE (LEFT AND ABOVE). SHE ORDERED CHAMPAGNE FOR THE PRESS AND SAID, "I TALK SO LITTLE FOR PUBLICA-TION BECAUSE I'M SO INDISCREET."

KEEP
THIS DOOR
CLEAR

HEPBURN RELAXED ON THE SET OF *ALICE ADAMS* IN 1935 WITH MORTIMER OFFNER, WHO CO-WROTE THE CONTEMPORARY COMEDY ABOUT A SOCIAL CLIMBER.

ING A GIRL WAS A TORMENT. I'D ALWAYS WANTED TO BE A BOY. JIMMY WAS MY NAME, IF YOU WANT TO KNOW. **"**

HEPBURN ON THE SET OF THE 1936 FILM *SYLVIA SCARLETT* (OPPOSITE) AND IN CHARACTER (ABOVE): "I HAD MY HEAD SHAVED AND FOR THREE-QUARTERS OF THE PICTURE PLAYED A BOY." THE FIRST SCREENING OF THE FILM WAS A DISASTER; THE CROWD IN PASADENA STORMED OUT.

"I am looking back and realizing what the truth was. The motives back of the action. I don't think it was all as cold-blooded as it sounds. I hope not. But the truth has to be that I was a terrible pig. My aim was ME ME ME.**"**

HEPBURN FELL IN LOVE WITH JOHN FORD DURING THE 1936 FILMING OF *MARY OF SCOTLAND* (TOP), BUT THE DIRECTOR COULDN'T BRING HIMSELF TO LEAVE HIS WIFE. IN 1937 HEPBURN WAS ROMANCED BY FRANCHOT TONE (CENTER) IN THE FILM *QUALITY STREET.* (OFF-SCREEN, SHE'D RECENTLY LOST THE LOVE OF LELAND HAYWARD, WHO HAD FALLEN FOR MARGARET SULLAVAN.) IN *STAGE DOOR* (BOTTOM, WITH ANDREA LEEDS) SHE PLAYED AN ACTRESS DESPISED BY OTHER ACTRESSES. *BRINGING UP BABY* (OPPOSITE) WAS SHELVED BY RKO IN 1938 UNTIL HEPBURN'S BEAU, HOWARD HUGHES, BAILED THE FILM OUT.

LESTER GLASSNER COLLECTION/NEAL PETERS

THE KOBAL COLLECTION

BURT GLINN/MAGNUM PHOTOS

A s long as I live, I will never forget the first day she appeared on the lot," the writer Adela Rogers St. John recalled. "We beheld a tall, skinny girl entirely covered with freckles and wearing the most appalling and incredible clothes I have ever seen in my life. Mr. Selznick swallowed a chicken wing whole." Ah, but others saw past the freckles and frocks. The director Rouben Mamoulian, who saw Hepburn before she'd even made a film, could tell that her face was right for the camera: wide, lustrous, geometric with cheekbones. "There are some faces that project the light," he said. "Hers does." Captivated by Hepburn's "luminosity," he immediately began seeking parts for her.

The first order of business on the RKO lot was, obviously, to ditch the suit that a friend had bought for Hepburn. Then her hair was straightened and her freckles covered with thick pancake makeup. (The freckles would lie buried for years; if any peeked through in studio portraits—like the ones seen here—they were hunted down and airbrushed.) The camera clicked, and soon everyone at RKO saw what Mamoulian had already perceived: a strong, alluring, made-for-the-big-screen presence.

The Look

That Katharine Hepburn is remembered as a woman of great dignity is something close to miraculous, considering what several costumers forced her to wear. Counterclockwise, from top left: Onstage, as Cleopatra in a 1960 production of *Antony and Cleopatra,* she teetered on the ridiculous, as she did when dressed as a Mexican in a publicity still for *Morning Glory* (1933) and in her *Sylvia Scarlett* knave-of-hearts suit (1936). Her aviatrix outfit for the 1933 film *Christopher Strong* wasn't bad, nor was the generic Hepburn gown, always a flowing affair, that she wore in *The Philadelphia Story* (1940). But why, oh, why did *Strong*'s designers then send her to the costume ball dressed as a gold bug? On the opposite page is evidence of what tended to happen when a wardrobe department, faced with the elegant perfection of Hepburn's body, for some reason piled on extravagant and ultimately distracting costumes. The offenders in this case were the costumers for the 1969 bomb *The Madwoman of Chaillot.*

MARTHA HOLMES

PHOTOFEST

THE KOBAL COLLECTION

LASZLO WILLINGER/MPTV

GLOBE PHOTOS

RKO/MPTV

The Look

Ultimately, no matter how much makeup was piled on or how egregiously tasteless the costumes were, Katharine Hepburn's wickedly intelligent spirit burst through. She not only had the Look, she *was* the Look. Though she obviously said plenty in her many, many roles, even when silent she was massively expressive. The Look gathered in her eyes, was aimed by her strong chin and hit the audience squarely. Cary Grant said of Hepburn, "She can see right through the nonsense in life," and this was her impossible-to-misread message. It came across even in stills, as here, top to bottom, from the classics *Bringing Up Baby,* with Grant (1938); *Stage Door,* with Ginger Rogers (1937); and *Pat and Mike,* with Tracy (1952). Opposite: The Look never faded, as evidenced here in 1984's hardly classic *The Ultimate Solution of Grace Quigley,* with Nick Nolte. ▭

63

Career
Part II

After a string of her early films failed to make money and won for her the sobriquet "box-office poison," Katharine Hepburn went home to Connecticut to play golf. She had a fabulous time. Who needed Hollywood? Then in 1938 she was shown a rough draft of *The Philadelphia Story,* a stage play with the elegant role of Tracy Lord written especially for her. "You're a goddess, Tracy. . . . You're lit from within, Tracy." Hepburn nurtured the play with its author, Philip Barry. She helped rewrite it, committed to performing it onstage and bought the film rights for $30,000. In 1939 she sold the rights to Metro for $250,000, with the stipulation that she play the lead. "Louis B. Mayer tried to make a tricky deal with me, wanting to put Norma Shearer or somebody else in it," Hepburn later recalled. The actress remained firm, and negotiations ended "with me getting my own way." But not in all casting decisions: If she'd had just a little more control of *The Philadelphia Story,* her collaboration with Spencer Tracy would have started with this film.

Nevertheless, what Hepburn accomplished was extraordinary, not least because she was a woman and the year was 1940. She deftly, determinedly orchestrated her own comeback, which not only salvaged her career but also returned her to Hollywood in a far more powerful position than the one she had held. She would never again be perceived as anything but a star, and as the years and the films piled up, she became known as a risktaker and an actress of remarkable range. From the romantic comedies to the classics to her great "spinster" movies, kicked off by *The African Queen,* she continually raised the bar. She took chances on all kinds of different roles, failing embarrassingly, succeeding brilliantly. Offscreen, too, she proceeded boldly. "Not me, boy! I don't want to get mixed up in anything like this," Spencer Tracy said shortly after meeting her. But even as strong a personality as his couldn't resist her. Hepburn was a force of nature, and she was going that way. Soon, so was he.

THE KOBAL COLLECTION

❝WHEN KATHARINE HEPBURN SETS OUT TO PLAY KATHARINE HEPBURN, SHE'S A SIGHT TO BEHOLD. NOBODY IS THEN HER EQUAL.❞ —LIFE, 1941

HEPBURN ACTED WITH JOSEPH COTTEN IN THE STAGE VERSION OF *THE PHILADELPHIA STORY* IN 1939 AND, OPPOSITE, WITH CARY GRANT IN *HOLIDAY* IN 1938. "IT'S SUCH FUN TO DO A REALLY GOOD COMEDY," SHE SAID.

HEPBURN TO TRACY: "I'D JUST MET YOU. YOU THOUGHT I HAD DIRTY NAILS. I THINK THAT YOU IMAGINED THAT I WAS A LESBIAN. BUT NOT FOR LONG. DID YOU."

" There are women and there are women—and then there is Kate. There are actresses and actresses—then there is Hepburn. She is wedded to her vocation as a nun is to hers, and as competitive in acting as Sonja Henie was in skating. If Katharine Hepburn made up her mind to become a runner, she'd be the first woman to break the four-minute mile. " —DIRECTOR FRANK CAPRA

BOB LANDRY

HEPBURN EXHIBITED HER CYCLING PROWESS ON THE SET OF *THE SEA OF GRASS* IN 1947 AND DISPLAYED HER SOCIAL GRACES (ALONGSIDE LENA HORNE) AT MGM STUDIO'S 25TH ANNIVERSARY DINNER IN 1949. TRACY IS IN THE BACKGROUND, NEXT TO FRANK SINATRA.

❝HE LIKED TO DRINK. HE DRANK. TO PUT IT SIMPLY: THERE WAS NO BUNK ABOUT BOGIE. HE WAS A MAN.❞

Oᴺ THE SET OF *THE AFRICAN QUEEN* IN 1951, HEPBURN COMMUNED WITH HUMPHREY BOGART AND WITH HER MIRROR, OPPOSITE. "EVERYONE SQUALLED ABOUT THIS MIRROR," SHE WROTE IN HER BOOK ON THE MAKING OF THE MOVIE. "DAILY IT HAD TO BE TAKEN FROM MY HUT TO THE CAR. DOWNHILL TO THE BOAT. TO THE JUNGLE. BACK TO THE BOAT. UP THE HILL INTO THE CAR AGAIN. TO MY HUT. AND EVERYONE USED IT. OH YES, ESPECIALLY BOGIE."

"All I can say is, I could never be anyone else. I don't want to be anyone else, and I've never regretted what I've done in my life even though I've had my nose broken a few times doing it."

HEPBURN FAILED TO CLOSE HER EYES WHILE FALLING INTO A VENICE CANAL IN 1955 FOR *SUMMERTIME*, AND SHE PAID FOR IT WITH AN EYE INFECTION THAT PLAGUED HER THE REST OF HER LIFE. SHE PREFERRED DOING HER OWN STUNTS BECAUSE, SHE SAID, THE STUNTWOMEN NEVER STOOD UP STRAIGHT ENOUGH.

"NOT MUCH MEAT ON 'ER, BUT WHAT THERE IS, IS CHERCE!"
—SPENCER TRACY AS MIKE, IN *PAT AND MIKE*

HEPBURN WAS A SUPERB GOLFER—SKILLED AND HIGHLY COMPETITIVE—WHO GOT TO DEMONSTRATE HER FORM IN *PAT AND MIKE* IN 1952. IN 1958, AS SHE ENTERED HER FIFTIES, SHE STILL RADIATED HEALTH AND ATHLETICISM (OPPOSITE). "I WAS STANDING ON MY HEAD THE OTHER DAY AND I GOT TO THINKING HOW PROBABLY UNUSUAL IT IS FOR SOMEONE OF MY AGE TO DO THIS," SHE WROTE AT 84.

"She would never let me show her anything. Yet she would understand so much. I'd tell her emotionally what I was going for, and then she would be wonderful. I eventually learned how to block her in scenes. I realized that when I asked her to sit she would stand, and when I asked her to go right she would go left. The thing to do was ask for just what I didn't want.**"**

—CHOREOGRAPHER MICHAEL BENNETT

THESE SCENES ARE FROM *THE IRON PETTI-COAT*, A 1956 REMAKE OF *NINOTCHKA* STARRING HEPBURN AND ROBERT HELPMANN. HEPBURN PLAYED A RUSSIAN AIR FORCE CAPTAIN WHO IS SEDUCED BY SPIRITS, PARIS AND A MAN'S LOVE. EARLIER, SHE HAD ALSO PLAYED WOMEN WHO WERE DRUNK, TO HUMOROUS EFFECT, IN BOTH *DESK SET* AND *THE PHILADELPHIA STORY*. AS DRUG-ADDICTED MARY TYRONE IN A 1962 PRODUCTION OF O'NEILL'S *A LONG DAY'S JOURNEY INTO NIGHT*, SHE SHOWED WHAT SHE KNEW OF THE DARK SIDE.

HEPBURN, FILMING *THE CORN IS GREEN* IN WALES IN 1978, TURNED THE HEADS OF LOCAL WOMEN HIRED AS EXTRAS. THE POLITICALLY OUTSPOKEN HEPBURN OFTEN CHOSE ROLES WITH EARNEST, LIBERAL SENTIMENTS; IN THIS FILM, SHE PLAYED A TEACHER WHO SAVES A POOR BUT TALENTED BOY FROM A LIFE IN THE MINES.

"WHAT A TREMENDOUS OPPORTUNITY IT IS JUST TO BE ALIVE. IF YOU CAN KEEP A-GOIN', YOU CAN WIN."

HEPBURN AND WAYNE, WHO WERE SCANDALIZED BY EACH OTHER'S POLITICS, FLIRTED ON THE SET OF *ROOSTER COGBURN* IN 1975 (ABOVE). IN 1981 SHE FILMED *ON GOLDEN POND* WITH HENRY FONDA (OPPOSITE). HEPBURN HAD JUST UNDERGONE ROTATOR CUFF SURGERY AND HAD BEEN WARNED NOT TO WORK FOR THREE MONTHS. BUT FONDA'S TIME WAS RUNNING OUT, AND HE WANTED HER FOR THE ROLE.

"Well, who is happy?—I am happy. I have a happy nature—I like the rain—I like the sun—the heat—the cold—the mountains—the sea—the flowers, the—Well, I like life and I've been so lucky. Why shouldn't I be happy?"

WITHIN A YEAR OF HAVING NEARLY SEVERED HER FOOT IN A CAR ACCIDENT, HEPBURN WAS RIDING A MOTORCYCLE WITH NICK NOLTE FOR THE 1984 FILM *THE ULTIMATE SOLUTION OF GRACE QUIGLEY.* "I'D LIKE TO SELL MYSELF AS AN OBJECT AS LONG AS IT'S PRACTICAL," SHE WROTE LATE IN LIFE. "I MEAN, I'M IN A BUSINESS WHERE I SELL MYSELF." □

Retirement

She was so ambitious, she once boasted, "I'm going to be the greatest actress in the world." Producer Stanley Kramer said of the hard-driving star, "She can work until everybody drops." And yet, Katharine Hepburn seemed perfectly happy when she wasn't working. She had walked away from Hollywood before—in 1938—and had enjoyed a wonderful hiatus, golfing and simply hanging out with her family. Yes, she had relished the resumption of her career, but dropping out of the business again—to nurse Spencer Tracy in the '60s—had suited her too. "I was peaceful and hoping that he would live forever," she said. "We grew orchids. And I painted. Badly. Fun, though." After Tracy died, she threw herself back into work. She made eight more movies, four films for television and starred in two plays and a musical before retiring for good in 1994.

She settled into Fenwick, her family's Connecticut beach house, and with typical Yankee bluntness she acknowledged, "It's so endless to be old. It's too god-damned bad that you're rotting away. Really, it's a big bore for anyone with half a brain. But you have to face it, and how you do it is a challenge." She faced it by embracing the natural world—taking long walks along the beach, tending the shrubs, plunging into the frigid ocean.

Two memoirs were produced for Knopf during her twilight years: *The Making of the African Queen, or How I Went to Africa with Bogart, Bacall and Huston and Almost Lost My Mind,* which she wrote at 77; and *Me,* which was published when she was 84. *Me* was a thank-you note to all the people who had helped her and loved her, and a final farewell to all those she had buried.

It was also a celebration of the simple life she loved so dearly: "Every Sunday when we were kids, we used to go flower hunting. I remember the walks especially in Hartford. Dad would pile us all into the car. Rain or shine, off we'd go. To the reservoirs, the woods, the mountains . . ." At Fenwick, Hepburn revisited those times and places, if only in her mind.

"KEEP A-GOING, GOING. THE QUESTION IS, WHEN COMES 'GONE'?"

PHOTOGRAPHS BY **JOHN BRYSON**

HEPBURN COLLECTED FOUR OSCARS FOR BEST ACTRESS—STILL THE RECORD. SHE WON FOR *MORNING GLORY* (1933), *GUESS WHO'S COMING TO DINNER* (1967), *THE LION IN WINTER* (1968) AND *ON GOLDEN POND* (1981). HER GOLDEN YEARS WERE SPENT MAINLY AT FEN-WICK (OPPOSITE).

IN THOSE DAYS, I WAS YOUNG AND PLAYING MEDIOCRE TENNIS. NOW I'M OLD AND WITH A FAKE HIP AND
.AYING MEDIOCRE TENNIS. **"**

IN 1981, HEPBURN KEPT
ACTIVE ON HER COURT
AND UP A TREE, WHERE SHE
DID SOME PRUNING. "I'M MORE
INTERESTING NOW," SHE SAID.

HEPBURN AT 80 WAS STILL ORDERING HER LIFE AND HANDLING WHATEVER NEEDED TO BE HANDLED, INCLUDING THE LAUNDRY, WHICH SHE DRIED BY SPREADING ON THE LAWN. THROUGHOUT HER LIFE, HER CLOTHES WERE USUALLY BAGGY—SHE USED TO WEAR HER LARGE SWEATERS PINNED IN BACK—AND SOMETIMES TORN. "I MAY LOOK ODD WALKING ACROSS CLARIDGE'S LOBBY," SHE WROTE IN 1987, REMINISCING ABOUT HER DAYS FILMING *THE AFRICAN QUEEN*. "BUT I'M THE HEIGHT OF CHIC IN THE JUNGLE."

"I never got very close to anyone in the theatre or movies. I suppose it was because I was a member of a big family and I always tried to get enough sleep. It sounds odd today when people say, 'What was he like?' and I have to answer I honestly don't know. But there it is."

" From my bed I see the sun rise. Across a field of marsh grass. Birds circling. A family of white egrets. Swans go honking by. I see the path of the rising sun gradually shift to the south as winter comes creeping in. Time is passing. Yes. Don't waste it. **"**

A N ACTIVE OCTOGENARIAN: HEPBURN HAULED FIRE-WOOD; PRACTICED PIANO WITH FRIEND LAURA FRATTI; PLAYED PARCHEESI WITH BROTHER DICK, SECRETARY PHYLLIS WILBOURN AND FRIEND VIRGINIA HARRINGTON. BOTTOM RIGHT: HEPBURN SMILED GRACIOUSLY WHILE HER SIGNS DELIVERED THE MESSAGE.

PLEASE GO AWA

KEEP OUT

DURING THE FILMING OF *ON GOLDEN POND* IN 1981, HEPBURN WOULD GET UP AT 4:30 A.M. TO WASH AND CURL HER LONG HAIR, AND THEN SHE'D READ THE SCRIPT. SHE CRAMMED AS MUCH AS SHE COULD INTO EACH DAY AND CLAIMED NOT TO BE TROUBLED BY THE PROSPECT OF DEATH. "WHAT RELEASE!" SHE SAID. "TO SLEEP IS THE GREATEST JOY THERE IS."

In Memoriam

Katharine Houghton Hepburn
1907–2003

❝The thing about life is that you must survive. Life is going to be difficult, and dreadful things will happen. What you do is to move along, get on with it, and be tough. Not in the sense of being mean to others, but tough with yourself and making a deadly effort not to be defeated.**❞**

THINGS LEFT BEHIND (OPPOSITE, CLOCKWISE FROM TOP LEFT): "A HAT FOR EACH PICTURE"; CURLERS THAT HEPBURN MADE HERSELF WITH ROLLED NEWSPAPERS; CANES AND CLUBS; SENSIBLE SHOES. ABOVE: THE MOTTO INSCRIBED ON THE FIREPLACE OF THE SECOND HEPBURN FAMILY HOME IN HARTFORD WAS PRESERVED IN STITCHERY. ▭

Just One More

In a late 1920s production at Bryn Mawr, the undergrad Katharine Houghton Hepburn made a lovely, demure Pandora. But she was hardly shy. As she later recalled about her younger self, "I am terribly afraid I just assumed I'd be famous." All of Hepburn's most audacious assumptions were realized during her dramatic, glorious life.   ☐